D0933525

HIP and HOP

Written by Gerald Hawksley
Illustrated by Colin King

B. Mitchell

This is Hip.
Hip lives in a pond.

This is Hop.
Hop lives in a burrow.

"Hip and Hop hop everywhere," says the owl.

"I can hop higher than anyone," boasts Hop to Hip.

"I could hop
over the moon!"
shouts Hip.

"I could hop over the sun!" shouts Hop.

"On your marks!" calls the hedgehog.

"I'll win!" cries Hip,
hopping over
two ducks.

"No one can beat me!" cries Hop, hopping over three hens.

"Hop, hop, hooray!" cries the hedgehog.

"Be careful, Hip and Hop!" calls the owl.

Hip hops over a hedge.

Hop hops
over a fence.

"Look at Hip and
Hop," cries Clara
Cow.

"I wish I could
hop like that," says
the hedgehog.

YIPEEE! Hop leaps over Henry Horse.

YAHOO! Hip bounds over Clara Cow.

Hip is zooming
through the air.

"Look where
you're hopping,"
calls the hedgehog.

Hop is tumbling towards the ground.

"Hip and Hop are hopping mad!" laughs the owl.

Hop's friends
are laughing.

Hop has landed
in Hip's pond.

Hip's friends
are laughing.

Hip has landed
in Hop's burrow.

"Silly Hip! Silly
Hop!" says the
hedgehog.